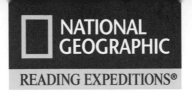

PLANET PROTECTORS

Waste Watchers

By Barbara Keeler
Illustrated by Margaret Freed

PICTURE CREDITS

3 (top left), 3 (bottom right), 5 (bottom left),
5 (right), 44 (top left), 45 (right), 46 (top
left), 46 (bottom), 48 (top left), 48 (bottom)
© Photodisc Green/Getty Images; 3 (top
right), 4 (top right), 44 (top right), 47 (top),
48 (top right) © Corbis; 44 (bottom) Mapping
Specialists, Ltd.; 45 (top) © Tim Fitzharris/
Minden Pictures; 46 © Philippe Clement/
Nature Picture Library; 48 (center) Ecosystems
by Nancy Finton, photo © D. Robert & Lorri
Franz/Corbis.

PUBLISHED BY THE NATIONAL
GEOGRAPHIC SOCIETY

Produced through the worldwide resources
of the National Geographic Society, John M.
Fahey, Jr., President and Chief Executive
Officer; Gilbert M. Grosvenor, Chairman of
the Board.

PREPARED BY NATIONAL GEOGRAPHIC
SCHOOL PUBLISHING

Sheron Long, Chief Executive Officer; Samuel
Gesumaria, President; Francis Downey, Vice
President and Publisher; Richard Easby,
Editorial Manager; Anne M. Stone, Editor;
Margaret Sidlosky, Director of Design and
Illustrations; Jim Hiscott, Design Manager;
Cynthia Olson, Ruth Ann Thompson, Art
Directors; Matt Wascavage, Director of
Publishing Services; Lisa Pergolizzi,
Production Manager.

MANUFACTURING AND QUALITY CONTROL

Christopher A. Liedel, Chief Financial Officer;
Phillip L. Schlosser, Vice President; Clifton M.
Brown III, Director.

CONSULTANT

Mary Anne Wengel

BOOK DESIGN

Steve Curtis Design, Inc.

Published by the National Geographic Society
1145 17th Street N.W.
Washington, D.C. 20036-4688

Product #4U1005111
ISBN: 978-1-4263-5104-4

Printed in Mexico.

12
10 9 8 7 6 5 4 3 2

TABLE OF CONTENTS

What Is Trash?

Trash is all the unwanted things we throw away. It can be a wad of paper you throw in the trash bin. It can be the food you leave on your plate. It can be a broken toy or yesterday's newspaper. All these things are trash, and they all get thrown away. We all know that a trash truck picks up our trash or we toss it in a dumpster. But then where does it go? Mostly it gets buried or dumped. In the United States we produce too much trash. Each person produces more than three pounds of trash everyday. Do the math. How much trash do you produce each year?

Total Trash Created in the United States

Millions of Tons

250
200
150
100
50
0

1970   1980   1990   2000

What Is a Landfill?

A little over half of the trash in the United States goes to landfills. Sometimes you'll hear a landfill called a dump. That's because trash is dumped into a giant hole in the ground and eventually covered over with dirt. That is a landfill at its most basic. Modern ones are a bit more complicated than that.

Landfills are divided into separate pockets or cells. Clay or plastic lines a landfill. This keeps liquid from the trash from seeping into the ground. The ground around the landfill is checked for landfill leaks. When a landfill is full, it is covered over with clay and dirt. Sometimes old landfills are used for things like parks or golf courses.

Meet the Waste Watchers

David

At first, David Benson was embarrassed by his parents. They recycle a lot and there are recycling containers all over the kitchen. But he learns that trash is a big problem in the United States and recycling is important. He starts a group called Waste Watchers to encourage his town to recycle trash.

GLASS
BOTTL

Joy

Joy is David's younger sister. She is in 5th grade. Joy joins Waste Watchers for meetings after school. She knows a lot about the environment and the trash problem. In fact, she knows more than her older brother.

Rita

Rita might be a skinny girl, but no one is going to bully her! She is a good friend and works hard for the Waste Watchers club.

Kengo

Kengo is David's sixth-grade classmate and best friend. Their mothers are friends too. Kengo started the Waste Watchers club along with David.

Blanca

Blanca is the brainiest girl in the sixth grade. She knows all the answers. She can be annoying sometimes, but she is a good helper for class projects.

CHAPTER 1

How It All Began

The ringing phone pulled me away from the mountain of papers on my desk. It was late, and the rings echoed through the empty rooms of City Hall. As mayor, I didn't usually have to answer my own phone, but everyone else had gone home. I sighed, picked up the phone, and said, "This is the Mayor's office. David Benson speaking."

I brightened when I heard the voice of my old sixth grade teacher on the line. "Ms. Harada!"

"I've told you I'm Nori to you!" Even after sixteen years, I could not get used to calling my old teacher by her first name.

"How's the youngest mayor in the history of our wonderful town?"

"Like the old mayors—buried in paperwork," I said. "How's the best sixth grade teacher in the school?"

"When I figure out who that is, I'll ask!" laughed Ms. Harada. "Meanwhile, my class wants you to visit."

"Because I started Waste Watchers in the sixth grade? That was sixteen years ago."

"But they need your advice now. They want people to use fewer throwaway bags. In fact, they're making shopping bags out of old rags to sell at the fair."

"Does Jake still come to teach them how?" I asked.

"Yes," said Ms. Harada. "It's hard to believe he was once the bully who terrorized the school."

"Not hard for me, one of his favorite targets." I said. "Is there anything you haven't already told them?"

"No," she said, "but they need to hear that kids can make a difference, and hear it from a kid who changed a whole town. You're their Mayor and their hero! Tell them how it all started. Show them all the awards. Point out that environmental work later led to great jobs for so many Waste Watchers."

"Like Mayor of this town?" I said. "Okay!" I checked my calendar. "How's Wednesday at 2:00, Ms. Harada?"

"That will be fine. But, please call me Nori," she said.

I hung up and rubbed my sore eyes. I picked up my pen, but I couldn't dig back into the pile of papers. The Waste Watcher story was already playing out in my head.

I looked at my framed copy of the 1990 National President's Environmental Youth Award. Waste Watchers awards covered the oak walls of my office, but I kept this one on my desk. The photo beside it showed the President handing the award to me when I was eleven years old. His words still echoed in my mind: "You're showing that people can make a difference." I knew that was why Ms. Harada invited me to her class.

I took my scrapbook off the shelf behind me. I leafed through at least 20 newspaper and magazine articles about Waste Watchers.

I put the scrapbook back on the shelf. Then I flipped off the light switch next to the shelves. In the darkness, I watched the moonlight slant through the windows. My mind began to drift back to those events sixteen years ago.

I tried to remember how it began. I wasn't always an **environmentalist** like my parents. In fact, they embarrassed me. I was grossed out by their compost pile in the yard. I hated having my friends see all the recycling containers in our kitchen.

I guess the wake-up call came during 1990—the summer before sixth grade. My sister, Joy, was about to start fifth grade. Our family took a new route to my aunt's farm near Salinas. It cut through some wild, undeveloped parts of California. We drove past farms, grassy, tree-dotted hills, and patches of woods.

environmentalist – a person who is concerned about things that affect the environment

I loved to get away from towns and cities. My eyes were glued to the window, especially where trees lined the riverbanks or crowded into the valleys.

About noon, my dog, Jaws, put his nose out the window, sniffing suspiciously. After a mile, I smelled it myself—something faintly rotten. As we rounded a hill, I was shocked to see the valley filled by a mountain of trash. The hillsides had been carved to widen the valley. Trash stuffed the valley as far as I could see.

"Gross! Is that a landfill?" said Joy.

"Yes," said Dad. "It's about full. Soon they'll cover it with soil. Then they'll have to dig another landfill somewhere else."

"In another beautiful place like this?" Joy asked.

"Maybe. Or near people's neighborhoods. It's hard to find places to put waste," said Mom.

For the rest of the trip, I pictured trash filling every tree-filled valley we passed. Meanwhile, Joy babbled nonstop. She loved to read about the environment. Garbage was her latest obsession. I'd started calling her "Garbage Girl." Now she lectured me, her captive audience, about landfills.

"Do you know that garbage can last for hundreds of years in a landfill?" asked Joy.

It was a drag to have a younger sister who knew more than I did. She was like those brainy kids they put on TV. I usually tuned her lectures out, but I half-listened this time. She said the average American threw out more than four pounds of trash every day. I struggled with the math: four times 365 is about 1,400 pounds a year, times four. . . .

Joy beat me to it. "That's more than 5,600 pounds a year for a family of four."

About twenty miles north of Salinas, we turned west into the hills. The farm nestled at the foot of a grassy, oak-dotted hill. A line of towering pines ran up the hill beside the white pasture fence. As our tires crunched up the gravel driveway, Stella, Ben, and my cousin, Ray, rushed to meet us.

As soon as we opened the car door, Jaws bounded out. He raced from Stella to Ben to Ray and back again.

Later, in the kitchen, Stella handed me a glass of goat's milk. She knew it was my favorite. It was so fresh I could almost taste the clover. I could hardly wait to milk the goats the next day.

After dinner, I amused myself watching Joy try to help Stella clean up. I knew better. I had tried to help last year.

Holding a plate, Joy stared uncertainly at all the waste containers. Stella had even more containers than Mom and Dad. She had three just for food scraps—compost, chicken food, and pig food. Paper was split up into good paper for recycling and burnable paper for the wood stove. Other bins held returnable cans and bottles, colored glass, clear glass, recyclable metals, two kinds of plastic, and waste for trash collection.

It took Joy four tries to clean off one plate. Every time she tried to throw something out, Stella waved her off. "No! That goes into the chicken's tub." "The animals won't eat oranges peels!" "That eggy napkin will smell if you put it in the tub for burnable paper."

I hid my smile behind a napkin. As Joy's smile faded, mine widened. When it reached my eyes, the napkin couldn't hide it.

After running from bin to bin, Joy's mouth had drawn into a hard line. My sides were shaking. "Do you have any plain old garbage for the trash collector?" asked Joy. She held out a sticky plastic wrapper.

"Not much," said Stella. She took the wrapper and dropped it in a small paper bag of trash.

I rushed into the bedroom and cracked up. Joy followed me and plopped down on the bed. She wasn't laughing. "The worst part is that Mom copies everything she does," I said. "Our kitchen is starting to look just like this one. And that yucky compost pile. . . ."

Joy's head jerked up. "Mom does NOT copy her! They just care about the same things. Anyway, you saw that landfill. Aren't you proud that our family tries not to throw out much trash?"

She had a point. "Oh, maybe," I said, "when it's just the family. But when people come over I wish they were more well—normal."

"You worry too much about what your friends think!" said Joy.

The next morning, I woke to the crow of the rooster. After milking the goats and gathering eggs, I looked for Ray. I spotted him carrying a tub of food scraps and caught up. We strolled through the apple orchard toward the compost pile. Jaws trotted at our heels. On previous visits, I had avoided the compost pile. I was half-interested now.

"I hate to see summer end," said Ray.

"Not as much as I hate to see school start," I said. I picked up the stick Jaws dropped at my feet. My stomach tightened at the thought of facing Jake.

"Too much work?"

"No, it's this guy Jake. He moved to town a year ago and decided the school needed a bully. My friend Kengo and I are on his hit list." I looked at my knuckles. They were white where they clenched the stick. I hurled the stick so hard it surprised even me. It flew over the white fence into the pasture. As it flew past, a sheep jumped into the air and bolted. The other sheep galloped behind the first.

"When the brains were passed out, sheep were near the back of the line!" Ray laughed. I didn't.

Ray stopped laughing. He looked hard at me. "Has this guy beaten you up?"

"Not yet," I said. "Only one kid's ever beat me up."

Ray raised one eyebrow. "What happened?"

I studied the ground. "Well I took. . . um. . . his jacket. I wouldn't give it back to, er, him. I was just teasing. Then, well he got mad and hit me. . ."

I couldn't look at Ray. I hadn't told him the whole truth. The only kid who'd beat me up was a girl named

Rita. She was only as tall as I was and much thinner, but my jaw still remembered her power-packed punch. I dropped her jacket. She'd since become a good friend, but I had never teased anyone again. I figured if Rita hated teasing that much, others might too. Besides I didn't like getting hit.

We reached the compost pile. Ray dumped the coffee grounds, orange peels, and used napkins from the tub. He then picked up a shovel and put a layer of chicken droppings over the food scraps. He finished it off with a layer of sawdust and straw.

Finally, Ray then covered the whole pile with soil. "This keeps away the flies," he explained. Ray was in eighth grade and he liked to play Professor Ray with me. I'd never wanted to learn about the compost pile before. Today I paid attention.

"What about all the germs?" I asked.

"Well, we want those guys," he said. "They're called decomposers. You must've learned about the food chain in school."

I nodded, but I hadn't paid much attention.

"When plants and animals die," Ray said, "decomposers break them down into stuff that plants can use for food."

I nodded like I'd known all along.

"Decomposers break down the compost and it gets crumbly. Then it can be used for plant food."

"So farmers use compost for **fertilizer**," I guessed.

"Only partly," said Ray. "Compost also controls the amount of air and water in the soil. That helps keep the soil workable."

"Not bad for a pile of garbage and animal droppings," I said. "I guess that's why Mom has one."

"She probably wants to keep her garbage out of the landfill, too," said Ray.

For the rest of the visit, I milked the goats and gathered eggs, as always. This time, though, I also worked

---

fertilizer – a substance that makes soil more fertile

at the compost pile. I noticed things I had ignored before. Almost everything on the farm was reused. The milk was stored in used jars. Old clothes, sheets, and towels went into bedding for the animals. They were also used as cleaning rags. Weeds, leaves, and animal droppings went into the compost. Wastepaper was burned for heat and cooking. Stella even fed junk mail to the goats!

The day we left, Dad started loading boxes of colored glass, clear glass, drink cans, tin cans, and plastic into the back of the station wagon. "We can drop these off at the recycling center on the way."

Jaws jumped into the back of the car. He settled on top of a suitcase.

About 30 minutes later, Dad pulled up at the recycling drop. Jaws shot out the door as soon as Mom opened it. After twirling joyfully, he scampered off to sniff around.

I looked at the marked bins. "It reminds me of our kitchen," I whispered to Joy. We lifted the heavy lids on the bins. As we dropped the cans, bottles, and jars, each landed with a clank, a clink, or a clunk. Then we put the empty boxes in a bin marked "cardboard."

I whistled for Jaws, who bounded into the back of the car and settled in a space we left for him behind the suitcases. He slept until we were about 10 minutes from home. Then he woke up, lifted his ears, and sniffed the air.

He stood up, wagged his tail, and barked joyfully.

I was as excited as Jaws. I loved this town, and I couldn't wait to see Kengo. We drove through the tree-lined streets and turned on to Rose Lane. In the middle of the block, we turned into our driveway.

I opened the door and jumped out of the car. Jaws bounded out and began to sniff and explore.

The next morning, Kengo and I took our last summer bike ride. Our favorite moments were spent in the wild country away from town. We peddled along a trail through grassy hills. I breathed in the fresh, clean air. The sky was clear, and the sun beat down on my shoulders. I tried not to imagine a landfill in each valley instead of trees and bushes. At the bottom of a hill, we reached the creek that cut through the hills.

We dragged our bikes into a dense thicket of bushes and trees. Twigs and dry leaves crunched under our feet as we headed toward the water.

The creek flowed over and around huge, round stones. A dense cover of willows, eucalyptus, and oak trees shut out most of the sunlight.

We dropped our bikes and sat on some dry stones. I reached into my pack and pulled out two crisp, red apples. I held one out to Kengo. My teeth crunched into the apple, releasing the sweet, tangy juice. Food, somehow, always tastes better when eaten outside.

"I love your aunt's apples," said Kengo.

"I'll bring a couple for lunch tomorrow," I said.

"Great! Jake will love them," Kengo said, bitterly.

I didn't want to think about Jake. Not here, where the trees and bushes shut out the world.

"How long do you think it'd take to follow the creek to its mouth?" I asked.

"A couple of hours," said Kengo.

"Let's do it," I said. We wheeled our bikes back to the trail and began to follow the stream.

As we rode, I told Kengo about the landfill. We cheered up as I described Joy running from bin to bin in Aunt Stella's kitchen.

"We don't have as many recycling containers as my aunt and uncle, but we have plenty." I said.

"And your mom's got my mom doing the same thing," said Kengo.

"The longer they know each other, the nuttier they get," I said.

Downstream, the wet clean scent of earth and water gave way to a rotten stench. Drink cans, bottles, food wrappers, and paper cups lined both sides of the creek and floated in the water.

"There's food garbage rotting somewhere," I said.

"Whatever it is, it stinks," said Kengo.

"The whole trash thing stinks," I said.

Kengo picked up a soft plastic ring. "I saw a picture of a dead seal with one of these rings around its mouth. The seal couldn't open it's mouth. It had starved to death."

"The ring might've washed out of creeks like this one and into the ocean," I said.

Kengo looked at the creek. He made a face and shook his head. "This isn't fun anymore."

"Let's head back," I said.

We rode back in gloomy silence. Finally Kengo said, "I read that during the beach cleanup this month, they'll work their way up the creeks."

"Right!" I said. "And then you know where all that junk goes?"

"To the landfill," said Kengo, nodding glumly.

"The problem's not just litter, " I said. "It's all the waste we make and what we do with it. Every year we throw out more and more."

"You're starting to rant, dude," said Kengo. "Ditto everything you say, though."

I stopped, picked up a stone and threw it violently. It landed in the creek, splashing water on the banks.

"We study the problem in school," said Kengo, "but I wish we could DO something."

"Maybe our parents aren't so nutty after all," I said.

"Don't tell them that," said Kengo.

It was almost dinnertime when I peddled up the driveway. I climbed off the bike and wheeled it into the garage. When I opened the kitchen door, my mouth watered. The smell of onions and beef rushed to meet me. Jaws was sniffing the air, and hoping for a hand-out. At the stove, Dad was stirring his famous cowhand stew.

Mom was putting onion skins and carrot tops into the compost bin. I looked around at the recycling containers. Then I gave Mom a big hug.

With a surprised smile, she asked, "Did I do something right?" I smiled and shrugged.

Hungry and hoping to eat sooner, I set the table. I took some blue cloth napkins from a drawer. My parents wouldn't use paper napkins. I was starting to understand why creating less trash was important.

CHAPTER 2

School Begins

The first day of school, Kengo and I carried our lunches in used paper bags. A block from school, my mouth went dry and my knees turned to rubber. Jake and his two friends stood at the corner of the school grounds. They were jeering as a boy walked away crying. Jake spotted us. His wide, flat face lit up as though he'd been handed a gift.

"Well, if it isn't Davina and Kendra," Jake gloated. As usual, Bud and Rich wore sneering grins and said nothing.

"What's for lunch?" asked Jake. He snatched my lunch and Bud grabbed Kengo's. I reached for my lunch but Jake stiff-armed me away. I dropped my arm.

"Can't afford new lunch bags?" Jake opened my wrinkled bag. He pulled out my last two Stella apples and took a bite of each one. With an approving nod, he dropped them into his own bag.

Bud took Kengo's sandwich and dropped it in his own bag. Jake took my sandwich, inspected it, and broke it up. He scattered bits of sandwich and paper bag around on the ground, then he stepped on it.

A crowd watched from a safe distance. Jake lumbered off. Bud and Rich trailed behind.

My cheeks burned hot with shame as the crowd stared. Kengo's jaw was clenched.

Blanca, the brainiest and bossiest girl in the sixth grade, rounded the corner. "David, pick up your litter and put it in the trash!" she ordered, rushing past. I gritted my teeth.

We found our classroom. Bad news and good news greeted us.

Bad news: Jake and his two thugs were in our class.

More bad news: So was Blanca.

Good news: So was Rita. Her freckled face broke into a grin as we walked in. Ms. Harada was strict, but she made learning exciting. She had been my teacher last year too.

Only five feet tall, Ms. Harada was shorter than some students. Even so, she could stop a brawl from across the school grounds. One "Hold it!" would freeze two muscled sixth graders in their tracks. When she raised her eyebrows, put her hands on her hips, and fixed her gaze on us, we knew she meant business.

During social studies, we had a lesson on citizenship. Ms. Harada talked about how citizens could serve and help their community. She brought up different problems, and asked for solutions.

Blanca was always first to shoot her hand up. After Blanca answered a few questions, Ms. Harada gave different students a chance. As others were speaking, Blanca's hand waved impatiently. When she did speak, she surprised everyone with her knowledge and ideas.

Blanca was a pain, though. When Ms. Harada turned to the board, Jake mimicked Blanca waving her hand. Several students laughed.

"Okay," said Ms. Harada. "Your assignment is to read the newspaper. Write a report about a current event that is affecting our town. Tomorrow, I'll ask four students to give oral reports. You won't know which students until I call on them."

At lunchtime, Kengo and I walked to Manny's Market. We bought crackers, yogurt, and oranges to replace our lunches.

For the first time, I paid attention to the store clerk bagging groceries. For the shopper ahead, he used ten plastic bags for fifteen items. As we paid, the clerk reached for a bag. "No bags, please," I said. The clerk raised his eyebrows.

I turned to Kengo as we left the store. "Did you see all the bags he used?"

"The potatoes already came in a sack," said Kengo, "but he put the sack in a double bag—all by itself. A six-pack of soda had handles to carry it. He put it in a double bag—by itself." He shook his head. "I never noticed how many plastic bags we used before."

"Joy told me fish eat tiny broken down pieces of plastic that end up in the ocean. A lot of it's from bags. Then we eat the fish. We'll end up full of plastic."

That night I did my homework. I read in the newspaper that the city council would meet and discuss how to manage the town's trash problem. Our town needed to obey a new law. The article said, "Every city in California must cut the amount of waste it sends to landfills. They must cut 25 percent by 1995, and 50 percent by 2000. The city council invites all citizens to offer suggestions."

I wrote my report about the city council meeting. Joy lent me her books to find some background information about the waste problem. I wanted to give the kids a reason to care.

The next day, Ms. Harada called on me last. I summarized the article about the council meeting. I reported on the gross landfill I'd seen and how landfills sometimes **pollute** the water. I described the trash in the creek and the stink. Then I told them people throw out more trash every year.

After I sat down a boy raised his hand. "Doesn't some stuff we throw out say 'biodegradable'?"

"Who knows what the word biodegradable means?" asked Ms. Harada.

Instantly, Blanca's hand shot up. So did Rita's. Ms. Harada called on Rita.

"Bio means life," Rita said. Blanca waved her hand. "Blanca?"

"Degradable means it can be broken down. Biodegradable means living things like decomposers can break it down."

Ms. Harada turned to write the definition on the board. Jake pointed to Blanca using his hand to mimic Blanca's mouth opening and closing.

"Has anyone heard of the Garbage Project?" asked Ms. Harada.

Only Blanca raised her hand. She was bouncing in her seat. "The Garbage Project is a scientific experiment.

----
pollute – to make unclean or poison

Scientists dug into a landfill. They could still read newspapers that were 15 years old. They found hot dogs that were still whole."

The class responded: "Eew, gross!" "Yuck!" A hush fell as Ms. Harada's brows drew together.

"So, think about the meaning of biodegradable. Why didn't papers and food break down in the landfill?" asked Ms. Harada.

Blanca and Kengo raised their hands. Ms. Harada called on Kengo. Blanca scowled and dropped her hand.

"Maybe they need something living to break it down? Like worms and other decomposers?"

"Good," said Ms. Harada. "And why might landfills not have enough decomposers?"

Only Blanca's hand waved. "Most decomposers—like some kinds of bacteria—need certain things to live. Oxygen and water, for example. So maybe there wasn't enough oxygen or water in the landfill."

"Good, Blanca!" said Ms. Harada.

Then Ms. Harada said, "The city council is calling for ideas to cut the amount of trash we produce. Let's help. Work in groups of four. Do some research about waste management. Try to come up with ideas for the city council. Then present your ideas in a report."

Blanca always did good work, so everyone wanted to work with her. Kengo, Rita, and I lucked out. Ms. Harada put Blanca with us. After school, we agreed on garbage topics to research and divided them up. Then we went to the library and fanned out. Ms. Fritz, the reference librarian, was a big help. She brought us stacks of magazines and government fact sheets.

CHAPTER 3

Waste Watchers Is Born

A few nights later, Dad announced, "It's my turn to cook again. Who's for Buster's Burgers?"

"Slacker!" Mom smacked him playfully with a newspaper. She was out-voted, though.

Fifteen minutes later, we parked at Buster's Burgers. Buster's belonged to Rita's father. The smell of sizzling burgers set my stomach to rumbling.

Waiting in line, I watched customers pick up orders as if for the first time. Food was wrapped in paper and served on paper plates. Orders to go were wrapped in paper, placed in plastic foam containers, and then put into bags. Drinks came in paper or plastic foam cups.

I went to pick up napkins and a plastic fork for Mom's salad. Each fork was in a plastic package with a knife and spoon. Mom would end up throwing away the knife and spoon with the fork and plastic wrapper.

From our table, we looked at all the trash on diners' trays. "You know," Joy said, pointing with a french fry,

"A lot of stuff's made just to be thrown away." She dipped the fry in catsup.

"That's why I look at how much packaging a product uses before I choose which product to buy. It's also why I make you buy products that use recycled material in packaging," said Mom.

I nodded, biting into a juicy burger. "I guess that's why you have all the recycling stuff in the kitchen, too."

"Duuhh!" said Joy. Mom and Dad looked at each other and winked.

Suddenly, I remembered an idea from my research. "We should take our own cups when we go for fast food!" I said.

Mom's smile widened. "That we will!" she said.

We had to rush home. I had planned to meet with Kengo and the others at our house.

Jaws joyfully greeted each of my friends at the door. Blanca smiled and Rita whistled as they admired all the recycling containers. Feeling proud, I explained the purpose of each one.

"The whole town should visit your kitchen. It's a great example of keeping waste out of the landfill," said Blanca. I was beginning to like her.

We sat down at the kitchen table. I knew Joy would hang around, so I invited her to join us. I smiled as she rushed to find an extra chair.

Blanca reported first. "I read about cities that burn their waste. They then use the heat from the burning trash to make electricity. I really like the idea! It's one solution that solves two problems."

"How do they make electricity by burning trash?" asked Rita.

"The same way they make electricity by burning oil, coal, or gas. They just burn waste for the fuel." Blanca said. "But the technology needs to improve. The burning causes some nasty air pollution. Also about 10 percent of the waste burned is left over. The ash is really toxic. Sometimes it can only go in a **hazardous** waste disposal site. It's hard to find sites for hazardous waste."

"Landfills pollute too, though," said Joy. Blanca pointed at Joy, nodding approval.

"I don't think burning trash is the solution for our town. It's expensive to set up, and it causes pollution." said Blanca.

"According to this article," Kengo waved a magazine, "recycling can reduce trash by as much as 35 percent."

Joy broke in, "Recycling also saves resources and energy. If we recycle more, then industry won't have to make so much new stuff." Blanca nodded. I felt proud of Joy—just a little.

----

hazardous – something that is harmful

Kengo read from the article. "Some cities cut waste by half because they recycle and they compost." He looked up. "Some cities compost yard waste and food waste in a big compost pile. Then it can be used for gardens."

Everyone nodded. "But can our town get people to haul stuff to a recycling center or compost pile?" I asked.

"Maybe not, but some city trash collectors pick up recycling and yard waste at the curb," said Kengo. "Some places even fine people if they don't separate their garbage."

Rita shook her head. "This town can't fine people for not separating recyclables. They'd be at city council every week, screaming and hollering."

"Maybe," said Kengo, "but they might like to save money by recycling." He scratched Jaw's chest.

"I know recycling's important," said Rita. She held up a fact sheet from the Environmental Protection Agency. "I got this from a government agency called the EPA. It says even recycling takes some energy and makes some pollution. It's even better to reuse things when you can."

"Like bags!" I said. "The bagger in Manny's Market used ten bags to bag 15 things! What if everybody saved their bags and took them to the store to reuse?"

"That's a great idea!" said Blanca.

Everyone stared. Did Blanca just say someone else's idea was great?

Blanca looked around. "What? It IS a good idea!"

Kengo said, "My mom uses old jars and plastic containers to store stuff. Buttons, pins, beans, leftover food. She doesn't buy plastic bags to store things."

Joy pointed to the daisies on the table. "This vase used to be an olive oil bottle."

"You can reuse things at stores, too," Rita said. "At Bill's Natural Foods, Bill sells food in bulk. People bring their own jars and fill them with honey or peanut butter. He has beans and grains in big bins. Some customers bring their own bags and fill them."

"That's a great idea. Besides reusing bags and jars, it cuts down on packaging," I said.

Rita looked back at the fact sheet. "The EPA says the best plan is what they call source reduction. I guess that means don't make as much trash in the first place."

"I was just going to say that," I said. "Reusing bags reduces the amount of waste created, because the store buys fewer throwaway bags. Another thing, if we don't buy things with a lot of packaging, that's source reduction too. My mom only uses cloth napkins. She cleans the house with rags instead of paper towels. When she doesn't buy paper napkins or towels, it saves trees and energy, it also keeps paper and rags out of a landfill."

"Buster's uses a lot of throwaway stuff. Plates, paper napkins, plastic containers. I'm going to talk to my Dad about it," said Rita.

"We're going to bring our own cups," I said. "That's source reduction, too."

Blanca said, "It also helps to use things made with recycled materials. If customers demanded products made or packaged with recycled materials, we'd have a lot less trash going to the landfill."

"OK everyone." said Blanca. "Let's start by making a poster for our report. It will summarize our ideas for the class."

We all set to work to make a poster.

Rita sat back to admire our poster. "But these ideas won't make much difference unless a lot of people use them."

REDUCE-
Don't make waste in the first place.

REUSE-
Use empty containers; don't throw them away.

RECYCLE-
Use throwaways to make new products.

RECLAIM-
Look for recycled material in products and packaging.

An item came to me in a flash! "We should form a club!" I said. "We can work to get the rest of the town reducing, reusing, recycling, and composting waste."

"Let's call ourselves Waste Watchers!" said Blanca.

"I like it!" said Kengo. "We can get other kids to join."

"I'll join!" said Joy. "So will my friends."

"We'll figure out ways the town can reduce the amount of trash it makes. Then we can put our plans into action," Rita said.

"Okay," said Blanca, "let's classify all our suggestions. Actions each person can take, and the ones we have to ask businesses, the school, or the city to take." She picked up a pen. When we finished, we had a long list.

We decided to ask the school to put out separate trash bins for recyclables. I called Dad to the table and explained our idea.

Dad said, "I will volunteer to take some of the school's recyclables to the recycling center. I'll round up some other parents to help."

"It'd be even better if the town would pick them up," said Kengo.

After the meeting, Blanca hung around. She and Joy had hit it off.

The next day we reported to the class. Blanca and Rita displayed our poster and our chart. I told the class about my Uncle and Aunt's farm. I told them almost all the waste on the farm was reused. It was burned for heat, composted, fed to animals, or recycled. Then Rita talked about reusing things people usually throw away. Kengo spoke about recycling. Finally Blanca explained that the best plan was to make less waste in the first place.

Many kids asked questions. The last question was probably the most important. One girl, I can't remember her name, asked if there was anything we could do.

Kengo then stood up and said, "Yes. We can start with the school. We can put recycling bins around the building. The gardeners can start composting leaves, weeds, and grass clippings." He pointed to the poster. "We can all do the four Rs."

Kengo told them about our Waste Watchers Club, and asked who wanted to join. Eight hands went up. Ms. Harada liked the idea. She said Waste Watchers could meet in her classroom during lunch and after school.

That afternoon, Waste Watchers met. Joy brought some other fifth graders. We invited the school principal and the cafeteria manager to meet with us. They agreed that separate bins would be put out for recyclables. The gardeners would compost plant waste.

Waste Watchers elected me president, Kengo vice president, and Rita secretary. Then we voted to go to the city council meeting and ask for curbside recycling.

CHAPTER 4

Waste Watchers to the Rescue

At the city council meeting, the Councilers sat at a long table on a stage. A microphone was set up in the aisle.

When our turn came, we went to the microphone one at a time. First, Rita described the waste problem. "If all the trucks we fill with garbage every year formed a line, the line would stretch from Earth halfway to the moon." she said. A few eyes opened wider.

I described my aunt's farm, and how little trash the family threw out. I said the businesses and city could use the same strategies. Blanca explained how much yard waste ended up in landfills.

Kengo told them about cities that recycled or composted as much as half their waste. Then he presented our plan for curbside recycling. He also suggested that the city pick up yard waste and make compost. People could use the compost on their gardens.

One council member looked interested. She asked,

"Does the money made from the recycled goods pay for the cost of collection?"

The city waste hauler stood up to speak. "No," he said, "It pays for part of the cost. Curbside recycling usually costs the city something."

The city manager went to microphone. "We'd need a bigger waste management department to manage a recycling program. That would be expensive."

Several citizens warned the council not to raise their taxes or trash fees. "If you squeeze one more penny out of us, you'll never be re-elected!" warned one woman. A mutter of agreement swept through the audience.

A man said, "No way am I taking cans, bottles, and plastic out of my trash. You get one bag of trash! Period!"

Too bad our parents were all at a PTA meeting. Only Ms. Fritz asked for curbside recycling.

Two council members voted for curbside recycling. Three voted against it.

As we left City Hall, I said, "We need to meet! If the city won't solve the trash problem, it's up to us!"

"I'm going to talk to Ms. Fritz. I think she can help," said Blanca. She knew all the librarians well. When we left, she and Ms. Fritz had their heads together.

Waste Watchers met the next afternoon. I said, "What can we do?"

"The people in this town are great," said Kengo. "If we can make them understand how bad the waste problem is, they'll want to help. We just need to give them some ideas. After all, the law says our town needs to reduce the amount of trash it produces."

"Ms. Fritz writes a column for the town newspaper," said Blanca. "She offered us space in her column to write about waste."

"Perfect!" said Rita. Everyone agreed. We elected Blanca editor. The first column would describe the waste problem. After that, columns would explain how people could help.

We took turns writing columns. Ms. Fritz checked our facts. She did not find any mistakes!

After a few weeks, I saw a few shoppers take used bags to the store. Bill said more people were bringing their own containers and buying in bulk. Manny's Market reported that customers were asking for products with less packaging. Buster said a few customers brought their own cups and take-out containers.

Rita put a sign on the napkin holder at Busters.

Big changes took place at school. The janitor put out extra bins for bottles and cans. Waste Watchers labeled them. The janitor put special wastebaskets in the classrooms for paper only. Every day, parents picked up the recyclables.

The teachers told us to write on both sides of a paper. They asked city offices for their used paper. We used the backs of memos and letters for scratch paper and notes. Teachers and students reused their lunch bags.

Not everyone supported waste management. Sometimes we found recycling bins dumped and the recyclables mixed with trash. We were pretty sure who was doing it.

The cafeteria had begun to put out recycling bins. Before taking our trays and dishes to the counter, we dumped cans, bottles, and plastic into recycling bins. What couldn't be recycled went into the trash.

Waste watcher members took turns sitting by the recycling bins at lunchtime. When one was full, another one was put out.

One day when Blanca was on duty, I spotted Jake about to dump his recyclables into the trash can. Jake was facing me with his back to Blanca.

Blanca scowled at Jake's broad back. "Not so fast! First the recyclables!"

Jake wheeled around to face her. Blanca gasped as she recognized him. "What did you say?" he asked, cupping his ear. He bent down, his face in hers.

Blanca looked down and said, "Nothing." Her voice was soft and shaky. His eyes on Blanca, Jake dumped his

whole tray, trash and all, into the bottle bin next to her. He swaggered off, thumbs in his belt loops.

Tears spilled from Blanca's eyes and rolled down her cheeks. Rita walked up. "What happened, Blanca?"

Blanca was silent. A student drew Rita aside and whispered in her ear. As she listened, Rita's eyes narrowed. Her arms folded, and her mouth tightened.

"You should report it, Blanca," said Rita as we left the cafeteria.

"I might as well paint a bull's eye on myself," Blanca said, "I'd be covered in food every day, or worse."

"One reason Jake gets away with everything is that nobody tells on him," said Rita.

"A few people tried." I said. "Nobody's ever done it more than once."

The bell was about to ring. Ahead, a smirking Jake and his buddies faced us, blocking the empty hall. Rita marched straight toward Jake, her chin lifted, her eyes fixed on his. Jake looked away. He stepped aside as Rita swept past with me at her side. Then it hit me! I wasn't the only boy who had learned a painful lesson from Rita!

CHAPTER 5

The Town Gets on Board

Waste Watchers had made a good start, but we wanted to do more. At one meeting, I said, "Let's write a newspaper column inviting businesses and residents to make promises to cut down on trash. Then we'll publish their promises."

We took a vote. Blanca was chosen to write the column.

The next week, promises began to pour in. Manny's Market promised to carry products with recycled materials and less packaging. Some restaurants said they'd use cloth napkins and stop using throwaway dishes. People said they'd take their own bags to stores. They promised to start composting and to reuse bags, jars, and bottles. Offices agreed to use both sides of a sheet of paper. Buster's stopped putting hamburgers in plastic foam containers. Food that was eaten at Buster's was not wrapped in paper.

People wrote that they'd recycle if the drop-off weren't so far away. "We have to do something," said Kengo, sorting through the letters at a meeting.

"What if we open a recycling drop-off?" I said. Everybody answered at once.

"Good idea, but where would we put it?"

"Who'd take care of it?"

"What would we do with the recyclables?"

I waved for silence. "We can't answer these questions until we decide to do it. Once we decide, we can ask for help. Let's vote!"

The next day, I went to Bill's Natural Foods. I showed Bill the letters. "We want to start a recycling drop-off," I said, "We need a place to put recycling bins."

"You can use part of my parking lot," said Bill. "It's never full." He opened the back door and waved for me to follow. "See," he said. "You can label the bins. Then put them here by my own dumpster."

"What do we do when the bins are full?" I asked.

"Jay Light makes money selling junk at recycling centers," said Bill.

"Okay!" I said. "He can pick them up and keep the money he gets from the centers."

"Waste Watchers Open Recycling Drop-Off!" said the next column. People swarmed to the parking lot with loads of recyclables. Many stopped to shop at Bill's store.

Each day, the bins filled. Jay picked them up and took them to the recycling center. Soon, the bins were starting to overflow. We put out more bins.

Someone was still out to get Waste Watchers, though. One Saturday morning, my phone rang. It was Bill.

"You'd better come over," he said.

I raced to the store on my bike. When I reached the parking lot, my stomach turned over. The bins were dumped. The recyclables were mixed with trash from the dumpster. Glass jars and bottles had been smashed and the glass scattered. Somebody had poured oil and sticky, smelly goo over some piles.

I called Kengo from Bill's phone. In 30 minutes, Kengo arrived with five Waste Watchers wearing gloves. By 10:00, most of the Waste Watchers were in the parking lot, trying to clean up the mess.

Nobody knew how she found out, but Ms. Harada showed to help. She even brought extra gloves.

Everyone had a pretty good idea who had dumped the bins. At noon, the suspects strolled up. Ms. Harada was bending over a bin. From the back, she looked like a middle school student.

"Hey, Waste Whiffers," said Jake. "Messy, aren't you?" Bud and Rich snickered.

Ms. Harada stood up and turned around. "That sounds like an offer of help," she said. Her mouth was smiling, but her eyes had that look.

Jake looked down. His two buddies hung their heads too. They were caught.

"Well, er, sure," said Jake.

"I have just the job for you three." said Ms. Harada. She handed them gloves. Then she pointed to the most disgusting mess of sticky paper, broken glass, rotten food, oil, and syrup. On top was something slimy that nobody could identify. "This is your pile. I need you to take out what we can still recycle and wash it off. Then put the rest in the trash. Wipe out the recycling bins, and clean the syrup and oil off the parking lot."

Jake's jaw dropped. He stared at the slimy, oily, sticky, stinky pile. His buddies hadn't looked up since Ms. Harada put the eye on them.

For the first time, I was glad to have Jake around. The idea of cleaning up that pile had been creeping me out.

CHAPTER 6

Back to City Council

The recycling center was a success! We couldn't keep up with it. When Jay drove up each afternoon, the bins were overflowing. We had no room for more bins. We called a meeting to discuss it.

"I wish the city would pay to pickup recyclable stuff from the curbs." said Kengo.

"What're we waiting for?" I said. "It's time we asked the city council again!"

The next morning, Kengo left for school early. Joy, Rita, Blanca, and I walked to school. Our mood darkened as we reached the school grounds. My stomach squeezed into a tight ball.

Jake stood by a dumpster, facing Kengo. Rich held the heavy dumpster lid open. A group of students stood watching. About eight belonged to Waste Watchers.

I sprinted forward. I reached the crowd just as Jake said, "You can climb into the dumpster or Bud and I can throw you in. It's your choice."

Kengo was shaking, but he stood with crossed arms, looking up at Jake. I admired his nerve. At a nod from Jake, Bud tramped heavily over to Kengo.

Suddenly, I knew what I had to do. Blood pounded in my ears and surged through my body. I took a deep breath, stepped forward, and linked arms with Kengo. "Kengo isn't going into any dumpster without me!"

"Even better," said Jake. "Plenty of room for two." He reached for me as Bud reached for Kengo.

"Make that three!" Rita stepped forward and linked arms with Kengo. When she fixed her eyes on Jake, he dropped his.

"Don't just stand there!" barked Blanca, stepping forward with Joy. One by one, all the Waste Watchers stepped forward and linked arms. Jake glanced at his friends. Their eyes were on the ground.

Jake flushed deep red, staring hard at each of us. No one looked away. "You know I won't forget this," he said, "you won't always be together."

"Let's go," Jake said. "They're not worth dirtying our hands on."

Jake moved away, trying to swagger. Bud and Rich slouched away behind him.

Heading for class, I felt a foot taller. My friends were standing straighter than usual and walking with a new bounce in their step.

At the Waste Watcher's meeting that afternoon, everyone cheered us for standing up to Jake. "I've written a report for the principal," said Rita. "I reported every time Jake has bullied a student."

Blanca gasped. "He'll break you and smear you all over the school grounds!"

"I don't think so!" said Rita. She winked at me.

"Let's all sign the letter," I said. Everyone reached for the pen.

"I'll give a copy to Jake," said Rita.

As I watched everyone line up to sign, an idea hit me! "Let's start a **petition**! Our recycling drop-off proves that people want to recycle. I bet most people would rather have recyclables picked up at the curb than haul them to the drop-off. We should get them to stand together like we are now."

"If enough people sign the petition, we can take it to city council. I bet it will help persuade them to approve curbside pick up." said Kengo.

----

petition – a written request signed by people who support the request

Everyone broke into excited chatter. "I nominate Blanca as petition writer; she can write the best" said Joy, when the chatter died down.

Joy and I walked home together. "I feel sorry for Jake," she said.

I stared at her. "Are you nuts?"

"I'm friends with his sister. She's in my grade. She says that he bullys people to get respect and win friends. She also says he wasn't always this way. A few years ago, their family moved to a town on the coast. Most of the people worked at the town docks loading and unloading ships. They were all big and strong."

"So?"

"The boys picked on Jake because his father was different. He's a tailor. One day some boys were making fun of Jake's dad. Jake snapped and beat up a couple of the boys. They left him alone after that. Some losers even started following him around. To Jake, it was like having friends. He felt important."

"So when he moved here he did the same thing," I said. "He could've tried something else first."

"He's real nice to his sister," said Joy.

The next day, we put copies of the petition at Bill's counter. On each recycling bin, we taped a sign: "Do you want curbside pickup? Tell the city council. Please sign the petition in the store."

Rita's father kept a petition at Buster's. Waste Watchers took the petition door to door. Ms. Fritz kept it at the library. All the teachers signed.

Kengo wrote a column about curbside recycling. He explained how well curbside pickup had worked in other cities. It could keep waste out of the landfills, he wrote. He told people where to sign the petition.

That week, the newspaper received many letters to the editor. Only a couple of letters opposed curbside recycling. People also began to send letters to city hall, demanding curbside recycling.

The afternoon before the council meeting, we collected pages of petitions. Hundreds of people had signed. Rita and Blanca sorted the petitions and made photocopies to give out at the meeting.

At the city council meeting, the room was packed. Waste Watchers made sure they were the politest members of the audience. Excited babble mingled with muffled grumbling. A hush fell as the mayor banged his gavel. Kengo went to the microphone and asked for curbside recycling. I handed a pile of petitions to the mayor.

Many people came to the microphone. Most spoke about the need for curbside pickup. Only five people asked the city council to vote against it.

At last, the city council took a vote. Everyone voted for curbside recycling. After the meeting, the waste collector hired Jay to pick up the recyclables.

The next day, Ms. Harada said, "Let's act on some of your ideas. I want you all to make something useful out of trash. You can use this trash if you want." She pointed to some bags of used paper, jars, bottles, cans, stained, worn out clothing, and leftover cloth.

Over the next few weeks, we showed our projects. Kids made all kinds of useful things. Our favorite was a basket to use at the store instead of bags. A shy boy whose name I didn't know had woven it out of vines.

After class, I saw Jake watching kids gather around the quiet boy. They had never paid any attention to him before. Some even walked out with him. For a change, Jake was silent and thoughtful. He rummaged through the trash bags and picked out a piece of heavy cloth.

The next day, Ms. Harada called on Jake. He tramped

up to her and looked at the floor. He held out a cloth bag with a cloth handle. "It's for, you know, carrying groceries and stuff."

Blanca raised her hand. "How did you make it?" she asked. Jake explained exactly how he had made the bag.

Joy's words echoed in my head: "The only way he knows to get friends and respect is to bully people."

Some inner voice told me to clap really loud. When I did, the rest of the class started clapping too.

Jake started to blush. He grinned and looked down.

"Where did you learn to do that?" asked Rita.

"From my dad," said Jake proudly. "He's a tailor and makes all kinds of fancy clothes. He taught me to sew when I was little."

We invited Jake to join Waste Watchers. He accepted and taught us all how to make bags out of rags. We set up a stand in front of Manny's Market and sold them to shoppers.

Jake didn't change all at once. He still liked to get his own way and flex his muscles. When he started to play the heavy, we all let him know. We stuck together, and he backed off.

The Saturday before Thanksgiving, the phone woke me early. "Read the paper!" said Kengo's voice. "Read the paper right now."

I stumbled out of my room. Mom and Dad sat at the kitchen table beaming. Dad pointed to the headline. "WASTE WATCHERS Win National President's Environmental Youth Award!" The article explained that Ms. Fritz had secretly nominated us for the award.

In April the President would honor us in Washington, D.C. Ms. Fritz had collected money from people and businesses in town. She had raised enough for the trip. The whole town was grateful to Waste Watchers. This was their way of saying thank you.

We couldn't believe it. Going to Washington, D.C. Meeting the President. A bunch of kids being recognized for helping their community. It was like a dream.

The ringing phone snapped me back to the present day. "Dinner has been waiting since 8:00," said my wife.

I was afraid to look at the clock. "Sorry, Rita," I said. "I'm on my way."

I whistled for Jaws II. He jumped up and trotted to the door. He wanted his dinner too.

I headed home. I now had my story ready for Ms. Harada's class. I hoped they'd be inspired. Maybe they'd find new ways to improve the town like Waste Watchers had. After all, as mayor, I needed all the help I could get.

Recycling

Recycling is taking a piece of trash and turning it into something new. Plastic bottles can be melted down to become a park bench. Glass bottles or aluminum cans are cleaned and reshaped into new bottles or cans. About 30 percent of trash in the United States is recycled. City trucks pick up trash that can be recycled in some cities and towns. In other places, people have to take their recycling trash to a drop-off place.

Recycling isn't a perfect answer to the trash problem. There are many things that can't be recycled, but recycling does reduce the amount of trash that is dumped. Recycling also reuses resources. It makes useless material useful again.

Total Recycling in the United States

Millions of Tons

1970   1980   1990   2000

Composting

Composting is a way of helping nature turn grass, leaves, and some foods into humus. Humus is the organic matter found in good soil. Yard waste and food are put into a compost bin. The mixture must be turned over to let in oxygen. Oxygen helps living things called decomposers break down the material. The crumbly organic matter they leave behind contains some nutrients. It makes soil workable and helps it hold the right amount of air and water. Some cities and towns have composting programs. People compost at home, too. Making humus for soil is one way of reducing trash. Composting keeps some trash out of landfills, and it makes something people can use.

The Garbage Project

The Garbage Project is a real study. It was started in 1973 at the University of Arizona by a professor named William Rathje. Scientists had studied trash from ancient civilizations for a long time. Rathje realized that our own trash might tell us a lot about how we really live. Rathje got permission from the city of Tucson in Arizona to take garbage left out for trash trucks. He wanted to study what people threw away. He found many surprising things. For example people throw away a lot of food.

The Garbage Project studied landfills too. Many people thought that plastics and diapers were taking up all the landfill space. Rathje's study found that this is not true. Newspaper and other paper take up far more space. Professor Rathje hoped that his research would help find a way to reduce the amount of trash people produce.

Write a Newspaper Column

The story gives many hints about everyday things you can do to reduce waste. Skim the story and take notes. What ideas do characters in the story mention for keeping trash out of landfills?

There is much more to be learned about taking care of trash. Research answers to questions not answered by the story. Then write a column for a newspaper. Tell readers what simple things they can do to create less trash.

- Reread the story. As you read, take notes about ways to reduce trash.

- Research at the library or online. Take notes while you research. What new information about trash can you find?

- Write a newspaper column. First say why trash is a problem. Then give readers simple suggestions for creating less trash.

Read More About Protecting the Earth

Find and read more books about how people can help the environment. As you read, think about these questions. They will help you understand more about the topic.

- What things besides trash can hurt the environment?

- How can polluted water, soil, and air harm living things?

- How do scientists study the environment?

- What can people do to help protect our natural resources?

SUGGESTED READING
Reading Expeditions
Life Science:
Protecting the Planet